LET'S GO!

Ten Adventures Through West Central Minnesota

LET'S SAIL!

Our adventures begin at the Hjemkomst ship
that once went on an ocean trip.
It was built by a teacher, with help along the way.
It was his dream to sail it to Norway.
His children made his dream come true.
And now it's here for you to view.

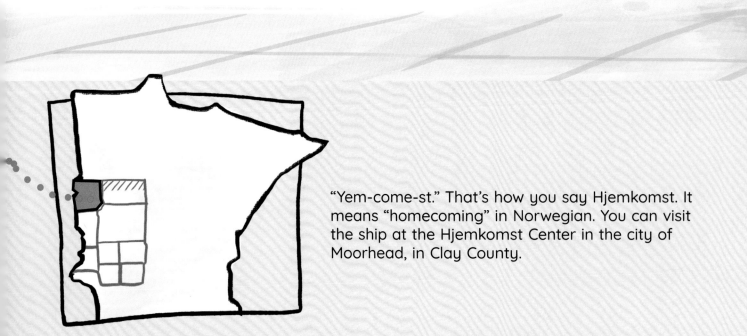

"Yem-come-st." That's how you say Hjemkomst. It means "homecoming" in Norwegian. You can visit the ship at the Hjemkomst Center in the city of Moorhead, in Clay County.

Activity:
Make your own ship! Have a grown-up help you find a box—one that you can fit inside works the best! Make decorations on the outside of the box. Maybe you even want to draw a dragon's head like on the Hjemkomst! Hop in the box—I mean ship! Now, where will you go on your adventure?

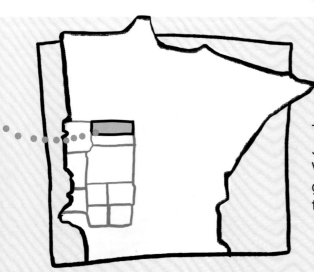

The White Earth Powwow traditionally is held each June. The powwow grounds are located on the White Earth Reservation. Attending a powwow is a great way for kids to learn about Native American traditions.

LET'S DANCE!

You will love the sights and sounds
at the White Earth Powwow Grounds.

Pum, pum, pum, pum!
That's the beating of the drums!

Hear the jingle of the dresses.
See the feathered headdresses.

Watch the dancers bounce and twirl,
each man, woman, boy, and girl.

Activity:
Here's an easy dance for you, just remember "one-two."
Clap your hands, one-two, one-two.
Bounce on one foot, one-two!
Bounce on the other foot, one-two!
Go back and forth. Now you're really moving!

LET'S SLED!

In wintertime, there's nothing better
than spending a day in the snowy weather.
Snow and ice mean lots of fun
for folks to sled, skate, ski, and run.
You can have fun in the winter too.
Just dress warmly, so you don't turn blue!

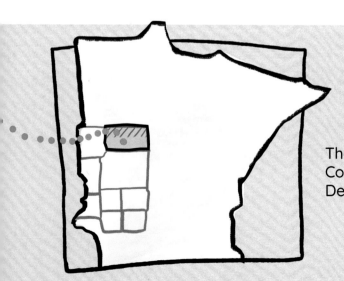

There are lots of places to go in Becker
County to enjoy winter activities. For example,
Detroit Lakes has an annual Polar Fest!

Activity:

It's snowing! Put on your snowpants and your warm coat. Pull on your boots. Got your hat, scarf, and mittens? Great! Now you are ready to play outside in the snow! You can make a snow angel by lying on the ground and moving your arms and legs up and down.

Did you know that Otter Tail County has more than 1,000 lakes? That is more lakes than any other county in the United States!

LET'S FISH!

Have you ever gone fishing? It's easy to do.
First, have a grown-up get a fishing rod for you.
Tie on a hook and a little bait.
Then, find some water—a river or lake.
Put the hook in the water, and when the rod bends...
Look! There is a fish on the other end!

Activity:
Let's count the animals in the scene above! How many otters do you see? How many ducks?

LET'S PLAY!

Let's go to a playground!
How many do we have in town?
This one has a climbing wall.
This one has a slide that's tall.
This one has a jungle gym.
This one has a pool—let's swim!

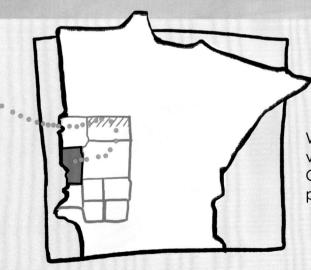

Wilkin County has many playgrounds to visit in its communities. From Breckenridge to Campbell to Rothsay, there are all sorts of fun places to play!

Activity:
Help a grown-up pack some snacks
and go to your favorite playground!
What do you like to do best? Going down a
slide? Swinging? Climbing? Jumping?

LET'S CAMP!

Some people love camping when summer is here.
They go to a campground with all of their gear.
They put up a tent. They fish, swim, and boat.
They nap in a hammock, or take a nice float.
At nighttime a campfire is cheery and bright,
where they can roast marshmallows under starlight.

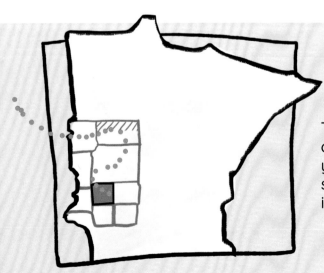

The Tipsinah Mounds Park and Campgrounds on Pomme de Terre Lake is just one place you can go in Grant County to camp or spend a day. You can even go camping in your backyard!

Activity:
Even when you are camping, it's important to brush your teeth before you hop into your sleeping bag! Get your toothbrush and put a little dot of toothpaste on it. Open your mouth wide and start by brushing the back teeth in gentle circles. Now move to the front, then brush the top, bottom, and all the sides of your teeth. Don't forget to spit out the toothpaste and rinse your mouth!

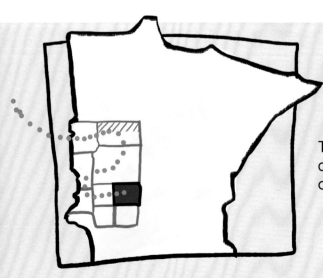

The Central Lakes Trail is 55 miles long and runs through Douglas County and the cities of Osakis, Alexandria, Garfield, and Evansville.

LET'S BIKE!

The Central Lakes Trail is great
to bike, walk, run, or skate.
There's so much to see
if you move fast or slowly:
farms, lakes, animals, and even Big Ole!
Drink lots of water and have a light snack.
Then, you'll have energy for the ride back!

Activity:
Let's move our legs! If you have a trike or bike,
you can go for a ride. Don't forget your helmet!
You can also run or skip or jump! Moving every
day helps your body stay strong.

Big Ole image used with permission.

LET'S BOAT!

Let's spend a day out in a boat.
On Lake Minnewaska, we'll paddle and float.
We will watch the different boats go past,
some go by slow and some really fast!
Over in Starbuck, if you keep a sharp eye,
you may even see a "dragon" go by!

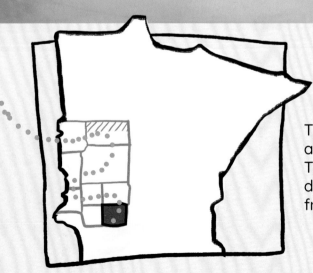

The Starbuck Dragon Boat Races traditionally
are held on Lake Minnewaska, in Pope County.
The boat is long—it holds 16 paddlers and a
drummer—and it has a dragon's face on the
front.

Activity:

Make your own boat! Save your juice box and your straw after you are done with your drink. Make sure you don't squish the box! Rinse out the box. Draw a triangle shape on paper and cut it out. That's your sail! You can color it and decorate it any way you want. Take your straw and bend the top down to make a triangle. Next, tape the straw to your sail. Have a grown-up poke a small hole right into the middle of the juice box. Put the straw in the new hole on the top of the box. Now, you are ready to sail!

LET'S GARDEN!

Up on a hill by a huge wind turbine
is a special garden. Let's see what we can find!
How many colors of flowers do you see?
Can you find a butterfly, caterpillar, or bee?
What kinds of vegetables are growing like they should?
Which leaves feel nice? Which plants smell good?

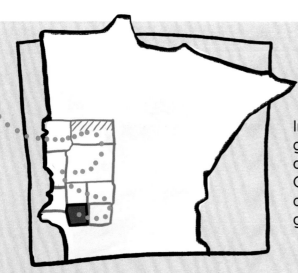

In Stevens County, the city of Morris has a children's garden that is part of the West Central Research and Outreach Center's Horticulture Display Garden. The children's garden includes a vegetable demonstration garden, a sensory garden, a music garden, a playground, and more.

Activity:

Let's make a salad! Help a grown-up wash some lettuce and your favorite vegetables. You can tear up the lettuce into bite-size pieces while your grown-up cuts up the vegetables. Put the veggies all in a bowl. You can add some cheese, or beans, or meat, too. Now, mix it all up and add salad dressing. Yum!

LET'S GO TO THE FAIR!

Have you ever been to a fair?
There are so many things to see there!
Cows, horses, chickens that might win a prize,
pumpkins so big, you won't believe your eyes!
There are singers and dancers, lots of fun games to play,
and beautiful fireworks to end your great day.

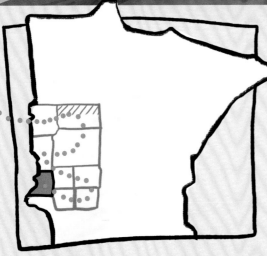

The Traverse County Fair is a great summer
destination for kids of all ages!

Activity:

What animals do you see in this picture? What sounds do they make? What's your favorite animal? Draw a picture of you and your favorite animal at the fair!

SPECIAL THANKS!

explorealex.com

SPECIAL THANKS!

hcscconline.org

WEST CENTRAL MINNESOTA
Early Childhood Initiative

EMPOWERED BY WEST CENTRAL INITIATIVE

ottertailcountry.com

This publication is partially funded with a grant from the Minnesota Department of Education using federal funding— Grants to States. Additional funding provided by donors to the Jeanette Jost Memorial Fund at West Central Initiative, the Inga M. Johnson Endowment Fund at West Central Initiative, Sam's Club, and the Morris Area Women of Today.

Text by Sheri Booms Holm and West Central Initiative.
Book design and illustration by Megan Hagel.

ISBN: 978-1-64343-727-9

Library of Congress Catalog Number: 2021917529

Printed in Canada
First Printing: 2022
26 25 24 23 22   5 4 3 2 1

Beaver's Pond Press, Inc.
939 Seventh Street West
Saint Paul, MN 55102
(952) 829-8818
www.beaverspondpress.com